Frankie Foulbowel's Bedtime Stories

By

Frankie Foulbowel

For Jeffy, obviously.

It's All About Frankie

Hello boys and girls. Are you tucked in comfortably? My name is Frankie Foulbowel the Famous Philandering Fox, although we don't necessarily use my full name all the time; partly because it's longer than a donkey's cock, partly because Mrs Frankie doesn't know about the philandering part.

I'm an urbane fox, *vulpes vulpes*, of the taxonomic order *carnivora*; clever, cultured, courageous, charming, but most of all, handsome. I guess you could say that I rock a 'loveably scruffy' look. My once vibrant orange fur, craved by aristocratic slappers throughout the ages, is a little faded and scraggly these days and my tail is somewhat short and mangled from an unfortunate incident involving an angry mother and a stoolpigeon crow. However, I'm still the tip-top fox in the whole damn woods. I'm actually the only fox in the whole damn woods, except for Mrs Frankie but she doesn't count. Speaking of my lesser half, Mrs Frankie would probably be quick to point out that I have deep digestive issues, hence my name; but what does she know, she's a fucking fox.

You're probably wondering how a fox is typing all this, right children? Well if you are, don't be stupid, I may be a talking fox with a stinking arse but I've still got paws and I am as good at typing as middle-aged white men are at dancing. I have kidnapped myself a baldling, one of your own whom I keep hidden and whipped. He does the typing, Frankie does the talking.

I'm the top boy in Gumpton Woods. It's a pretty little place where the trees are old and gnarled and in the summer they colour the sky green and shade the woodland floor with dappled, cool shadows that morph and shift with the breeze. In the winter our semi-sentient kin shed their summer coats, opening the grey drama of the unknown beyond to the curious gaze of our more existential residents. Gumpton Woods is surrounded on all sides by concrete, festering eyesores, full of you dirty baldlings doing your dirty baldling things, hurtling around in your dirty baldling killing machines and giving each other your dirty baldling diseases. We in the woods try to stay as far away from you as we can. Sometimes we

4

get visitors from the baldling world, they come walking to 'get in touch with nature' or to do things that they can only do amongst the dirt and the creatures. You'd do well to stay away, baldlings are not tolerated here. A while ago we had a few students who came to smoke crack and look at the pretty flowers. Bronson the Bodybuilding Badger did everyone the courtesy of stabbing them in the eye with a sharpened twig and stealing their hard-earned student loan cash, and of course their crack, which he kept to himself, as is Bronson's way. Personally I wasn't too arsed, crack is for badgers; I'm more of a mushies and herb kind of a fox. My baldling literary minion came to the woods one day to look for inspiration. He oo'd and ah'd and at all the pretty things and scribbled in his notebook. Fairy. Nature inspired him with a quick tab of Rohypnol in his tin of Stella while he slept, he was 'inspired' to be mine more quickly than Saucy Sally the Street Walking Squirrel can open her little squirrelly legs; but we'll get around to that diseased rodent ho-bag before too long.

Apart from occasional, ill-advised visits from junkie baldlings, drugs generally come into the woods through Bronson and

Samson the Pimp Daddy Beaver. Samson is Saucy Sally and Bianca Bunny's pimp and he hires those bitches out hard to any species that passes through our green and pleasant place. Make no mistake, Samson is shadier than Slim Shady's shady bits; a beaver so morally corrupt that he wouldn't be out of place in the Houses of Parliament. Except for the fact that he's a beaver. Now, children, you may ask 'how is it that you, a fox, are able to make so many cultural references about the world of baldlings?' It would be a fair question, to which I would probably reply: 'piss off, you nosy little bastards.' Although if pushed I'd explain that I am a worldly fox, a master of the vulpine arts; a fox so urban that one day I may release a ground-breaking grime album before selling out to make a quick fistful of mullah; *that* urban.

Being of keen curiosity and given my gregarious nature, I have, over the years, come into possession of a great many stories of the goings-on of Gumpton Woods. One could say I have tales of tails, or that I am a nature curator. I simply feel it is my duty as the brains of the animal kingdom to share these stories with you. Along this strange and worrying journey you will meet my pal Tweak, runt of a litter of hedgehogs, although he's not quite as defenceless as he makes out; then there's Touché, the inbred migrant turtle who was born with the wrong bits; Bronson the Bodybuilding Badger, Gerry the Catholic Caterpillar and of course, everyone's favourite street-walking squirrel, Saucy Sally.

So, baldlings, are you ready? Hold on to my paw tightly now because this could get scary. If anyone asks, just point at the dolly and show them where Uncle Frankie made you touch him. Yeah, right there.

The Tale of Tweak the Speeding Hedgehog

It seems fitting that I begin with the story of how I came to meet my partner in crime. My little smoking buddy; Watson to my Sherlock, Cheech to my Chong: Tweak.

Deep in the woods there is a clearing where there is a big, old oak tree with broad branches and a wizened trunk that is as wide as an elephant's arse. The tree trunk is split and rotten, making a small hollow where once upon a time there was a nest and in that nest a mummy hedgehog gave birth to three little boy hedgehogs. The first two came out big and strong like the daddy hedgehog who had scarpered as soon as the mummy had said those dreaded words: 'I'm late.' She named them Spike and Prickle, or Prick for short. But the third one was so small and weak that she didn't think that he would survive, so she didn't bother to name him at all. As the days went by the two strong hedgehogs made sure they got enough milk but the little one was pushed out of the way until he became twisted and malnourished, like baldling children brought up on pop tarts and

8

chicken nuggets. But however weak he was, he would still try and raise himself up on his spindly legs, even though he would shake like a shitting dog. Eventually the mummy hedgehog decided that if he wasn't going to die she'd better give him a name; she decided on Tweak.

Tweak's brothers used to torment him something terrible. They would pull his spikes out and wee in his eye, they even told him that he would get cancer from their mummy's milk. Now that's not very nice, is it children? One day their mummy left the nest and had an unfortunate meeting with a pizza delivery moped whose driver didn't come off much better. As she never came home again the three brothers had to go out into the big scary woodland all on their own.

Tweak's problems only got worse when they left the nest and began foraging for themselves. Everywhere he turned one of his nasty brothers would be there calling him names like cripple or retard. Tweak grew terribly poorly and nervous, he felt alone and unloved. All he wanted was a big scratchy cuddle from his mummy.

9

One day when Spike and Prick were in a particularly nasty mood, they told Tweak that there was a garden by the edge of the woods and that the nice baldling children who lived there put out a saucer of milky bread every night to help hungry hedgehogs. Poor little Tweak limped there as fast as his feeble legs would carry him while his brothers secretly followed at a safe distance so they could watch the fun.

When Tweak got to the garden he saw that there really was a saucer of milky bread. 'Wow!' He thought to himself, 'my brothers have been nice to me for a change. Maybe they love me after all!' He snuck across the garden, looking this way and that to check he was safe, before tucking into the milky bread with a big satisfied smile on his little hedgehog face. His brothers hadn't really lied to him, they just hadn't told him that the milky bread was a trap used by some nasty baldling boys so that they could hurt little woodland creatures. Now that's a cunt's trick, isn't it children?

The two boys came running out of the house and before poor Tweak's crippled legs could carry him away they started using him as a football. They kicked the poor little hedgehog all around the garden until they got bored and went inside to look at midget porn on the internet. My sad little sidekick limped back to the woods as fast as he could, which was about as fast as a slug that has taken Valium. He went back to the nest under the big oak tree where it still smelled a little bit of his mummy, and there he cried and cried while he waited to die.

Saucy Sally the Street Walking Squirrel had been out selling her bushy tail to passing trade so that she could please her daddy, Samson. He wasn't her real daddy, children, and if your daddy asks you to do that, be sure to tell social services. Saucy Sally had seen everything, she took pity on poor little Tweak and took him some food. She poked her head around the nest and found Tweak still crying like a baby that has shit itself. 'Here you go, batty-boy.' She said, pushing some worms into the nest, 'I hear that hedgehogs like to eat stuff like this.'

Tweak looked up at Saucy Sally with a face that shone with gratitude. 'Why thank you Saucy Sally.' He exclaimed. 'I thought I was going to die.'

In the following days the slutty squirrel kept taking food to her patient and soon he started to become healthy again, or as healthy as he was ever going to be. Eventually Tweak ventured out into the woodland once more and his brothers came to taunt him. They told him that they wished the boys had killed him and that he only had a tiny little cock. Surely it was only a matter of time before they did something horrific to him again! Saucy Sally worried about Tweak a lot, so one day she decided to ask for some advice from her wise daddy. Samson the Pimp Daddy Beaver thought long and hard, until he came up with an idea. 'I've got it!' He cried out at the top of his lungs as he pulled out of Sally giving her quite a shock! 'What we need to do ith get him hooked on thpeed.' He lisped through his massive teeth as he wiped himself clean on Saucy Sally's tail.

'Do you think that will help him?' Saucy Sally snapped, she hadn't come and was feeling a bit frustrated.

'Will it fuck!' Samson replied, 'But it'll be funnier than drowning kittenth!' With that he produced a large bag of white powder and gave it to Saucy Sally. 'Now take that to him, bitch, and I don't want no argumenth!'

Saucy Sally knew what was good for her, so she did as she was told and took the bag of white powder to Tweak as fast as she could. She found him in a bush nudging a piece of bark with his nose. 'What are you doing Tweak? You can't eat that you fucking mongtard! Try some of this powder.'

'What is it Saucy Sally?' Tweak asked.

'It's…erm…some magic pixie dust that a magic pixie gave me to make you stronger!' Saucy Sally replied. Now at this point, children, you might think that underneath it all Saucy Sally is a bit of a cunt and, if I'm honest, you'd be right.

Tweak apprehensively pushed his nose inside the bag. 'It smells funny Saucy Sally, are you sure it's safe for hedgehogs?'

'You'll be fine Tweak, I promise. Now sniff the fucking powder!' Tweak put his nose inside the bag and inhaled sharply. 'That's a good boy. Get a nice hit right up there.' Saucy Sally said affectionately.

He took his nose out of the bag; it had the white powder all over it. 'My nose hurts, Saucy Sally, and that stuff tastes all bitter and horrible. My head feels funny.'

Saucy Sally took his face in her paws and licked him clean. 'Don't worry honey. It'll all be ok. Now you stay out of trouble. You can keep the bag of dust. Just have more when it wears off. I've got to go and earn Samson some sugar.' And with that she scurried up a tree, fluttering her eyelids at a passing vole.

Tweak hobbled away in his usual fashion, feeling very strange indeed. But as he hobbled he realised that he was hobbling faster! In fact he didn't need to hobble at all! 'This magic pixie dust works!' He thought to himself. Or did he say it out loud? He wasn't sure.

Very soon he was rocketing through the undergrowth like a ferret on fire. He snuffled out spiders and wiggled after worms, all the while chewing the inside of his cheeks and grinding his little hedgehog teeth like a mental patient who's run out of Thorazine. As Tweak bolted into a small clearing he saw a little girl hedgehog that he had never seen before. As quick as a flash he rushed over and tried to jump on her back like the boy squirrels did with Saucy Sally. 'What on earth are you doing?' The girl hedgehog exclaimed.

'I'm trying to do the thing that everyone pays Saucy Sally for.' Tweak replied.

'Not with that fucking thing you're not, mate!' The girl hedgehog said and started laughing. Tweak looked down at little Tweak; lo and behold, he'd nearly disappeared!

'Oh no!' said Tweak. 'I have got a tiny cock after all!' Just as he thought things couldn't get any worse, Spike and Prick appeared in the clearing, they'd been watching the whole thing!

'Ah, what a cunt!' Spike said. 'He's got a cock like a pigeon's toe.'

'Look at that little thing, that wouldn't satisfy a sparrow!' Prick said, rolling on his spiny back and clutching his sides with laughter. Poor Tweak ran away as fast as his speedy little legs would carry him. Which was very fast indeed, children!

Eventually he stopped and sat in a bush. He sniffed a bit more of the powder and then some more. Then he left it awhile and sniffed some more until his poor little heart felt like it was going to burst out of his chest. Suddenly everything seemed fine again so he went for a little run, just because he could!

After running for what seemed like ages, Tweak came to the edge of the woods and found something very strange that he'd never seen before. It was a big flat surface that stretched away into the distance as far as the eye could see. 'What's this,' he wondered while he tapped his foot and chewed his tongue. 'Let's see what's on the other side!' Tweak started to scurry across. When he got halfway he saw something in the distance, two small, bright lights.
'Ahh…look at the pretty lights.' He said out loud. He stopped and stared, hypnotised as they grew and grew. A steady roar built, filling the air with trembling thunder. Tweak didn't know which way to run as the noise grew louder and louder and the lights brighter and brighter. Instinctively he rolled himself into a ball as the roaring reached screaming pitch, drowning out thought and fear and the amphetamine trembles.

'FFFFUUUUUUUCCCCKKKKKKKKKKK!!!!!' Tweak screamed as the air rushed past, making him move like a football in the wind. The roaring was everywhere, like the whole world had turned into one big shout. His heart was beating so fast that he thought it might explode. And yet as horrible and scary as this was, Tweak started tapping his foot like he was listening to music and laughing maniacally; that crazy, drugged up woodland creature!

As quickly as it had come the roar went away and the air around him stopped moving. Tentatively, Tweak unfurled himself from his protective ball. He tried to scamper away but he was shaking so much he couldn't move his legs properly. He was twitching uncontrollably and his front claw kept on hitting him in the face making it impossible to see or walk.

Just then a voice spoke from behind Tweak. Little did he know that his life had changed forever; he was in the presence of a legend. 'Easy now hedgehog, that was some pretty hardcore shit. You were playing fucking chicken with that car!' I said.

'Please Mr, can you help me?' Tweak replied, as bewildered as a mugged granny. 'My legs are doing this shaking thing and I can't walk.'

'No worries, my little friend. Frankie Foulbowel the Famous Philandering Fox is at your service. Now, for a start that thing there is called a road; stay the fuck away, yeah? But if you do get caught out there, stay between the lights. Between them!'

I helped Tweak back to the woods and as I did his strange twitching died down. When we were deep in the undergrowth we stopped for a rest. 'So, what gear are you on, little brother?' I asked, sniffing Tweak inquisitively. 'Hm? Green? Yayo? Crack? Brown? What have you been taking?'

'I don't understand Mr Foulbowel. What do you mean?'

'What drugs are you on boy! You don't get all twitchy and fucked up like that without pharmaceutical assistance.' I replied.

'I don't know what drugs are. Saucy Sally the Street Walking Squirrel gave me a bag of magic pixie dust because I'm a little pussy and the magic pixie said it would make me big and strong.' I pondered for a moment and as I did a large sound like a flock of starlings flying away erupted from me. Tweak wrinkled his little nose. 'Mr Foulbowel, that smell is disgusting!' He suddenly went a little green as if he was going to be sick. I assumed it was the shock and the drugs.

'Yeah sorry about that, it sometimes happens when I concentrate. Have you still got the bag of pixie dust?' Tweak handed over the bag of powder that he had been clutching. I dipped a claw in and tasted the contents, swirling it around my mouth like a connoisseur. I spat it out on the ground and grinned at a curious Tweak who had been watching with fascination. 'That fucking ho-bitch squirrel has been feeding you speed, my little friend.'

'What's speed, Mr Foulbowel?' Tweak replied.

'Speed is a bad drug, mate. If you carry on taking it you'll never sleep again but if you stop you'll want to kill yourself. It's a catch 22. Fortunately you've come to the right place because when you've got problems with drugs you have to talk to Frank.' Right children? Ha!

'This all sounds a bit scary, Mr Foulbowel.' Said the twitching hedgehog. 'Is there any cure?'

'It just so happens there is. All you have to do is give the bag to me and swap it for this one.' I produced a bag full of the herb of love and gave it to Tweak along with some Rizla and tobacco.

'What do I have to do with this, Mr Foulbowel?'

'For a start you can stop calling me 'Mr'; it's Frankie.' I said. I proceeded to show Tweak how to roll the herb into a splif. When we had rolled one each we sat back against a tree and smoked and smoked and smoked until little Tweak's eyes were redder than the devils dick. Wasn't that nice of me, children?

'Fuuuuuuuuck Frankie. That is some good shit.' Tweak eventually said. His voice had dropped an octave and his tongue seemed to loll lazily from one word to the next.

I grinned, I was beginning to like this prickly little scrote. 'It's all good, Tweak my main man.' I toked on my splif. 'So, what's your story bro?'

Tweak started to tell me all about his problems with Spike and Prick. I sat quietly and listened while he spoke. When he had finished I jumped to my feet, frightening our hedgehog friend. 'This is a fucking travesty, Tweak. We're gonna get our own back on those bastards for you.' I outlined my plan to him. The whole time Tweak nodded his head enthusiastically. When I had finished he sat back and laughed and laughed and laughed. 'What are you laughing at Tweak?' I asked; it was a good plan but not a funny one.

'I don't know, Frankie, but it feels fucking good.' He wiped his streaming eyes, accidentally poking himself with a claw.

I began to laugh too. 'Tweak, have you listened to a fucking word that I've said?'

'Not really.' He replied still giggling. 'I've just been watching your nose twitch while you talked.' Now we both descended into hysterics. While we laughed I decided that I was clearly going to have to sort things myself.

The next evening Tweak was starting to feel a lot better. He spent the day smoking herb in the nest under the big oak tree. Sleep was always going to evade him but I hoped that the weed would at least take the edge off the speed come-down. As the sun dipped low behind the horizon and the shadows grew long, Tweak tentatively poked his nose out of the nest. As soon as he did he saw his brothers chasing each other around, their eyes were as wide as saucers and they looked like they were foaming at the mouth. Prick's jaw was sticking out like it was dislocated and Spike's eyes kept rolling back into his head making him look like an extra from a zombie film.

'Ah, you little shit!' Spike said when he caught sight of his little brother. 'We got lucky and found a big saucer of milky bread right in the middle of the woods and we ate it all and didn't save any for you!'

'It smelt a bit funny but that didn't put us off!' Said Prick, his eyes looked like painted golf balls. Something clicked inside Tweak's head; he realised that I had given the speed to his brothers. Right on cue I stepped into the clearing. 'Yo, yo my hedgehog brethren, I got a little surprise for you. Come with me'

'Why should we trust a fox?' Spike said. Even off his tits he was a suspicious little bastard. Tweak had a flash of inspiration that for him was a stroke of near genius.

'I'll come with you Mr Fox, I want a surprise!' He said.

'Fuck that!' Shouted an excitable Prick. 'If that cunt's getting something I want it too!'

'Okey dokey then my scratchy trio of hogs, follow old Frankie. Best stay back though, I had curry last night.' With that I scampered away with the three hedgehog brothers following. Without the benefit of pharmaceutical enhancements and being more stoned than a Saudi adulteress, Tweak struggled as he always had. His brothers and I were soon nowhere to be seen, but still Tweak staggered on. Like I said before, Tweak's not as stupid as he makes out; he knew where I was going. Soon he made it back to the road where only the previous evening we had met. I grinned as he stumbled out of the woods and tipped me a stoned wink. I'd been trying to keep the two twatted hedgehogs busy but they struggled to stay still. They were off their little tits, children!

I waited until Tweak approached so he could hear what I was telling his brothers. 'Serious boys, if you wait over there some baldling is going to bring you some milky bread. I heard them saying it so I thought I'd help you out but if you ain't interested I'll go and find some hedgehog who is.'

Spike began an angry reply but Tweak stepped in. 'I want milky bread Mr Fox. What do I have to do?'

'My days, finally we have a hedgehog with some balls' I exclaimed rolling my eyes at the twitching pair. 'All you've got to do is wait over there and they'll bring it out!' I winked at Tweak again and hoped that he would remember my advice.

With that Tweak stepped out on to the road. Already in the far off distance I could see two pin pricks of light. Tweak shouted at me. 'I'm ready. Will it take long, Mr Fox?'

'Nah man, it'll be real quick.' I replied.

It all seemed to be too much for Prick to contain. He twitched and shook into action, skipping out on to the road and pushing

Tweak aside. 'Fuck this, I want the milky bread. You ain't having none, you little shit!' Prick said.

This seemed to galvanise Spike into action and he ran out as well. 'Fuck off Tweak or I'll kill you.' He spat viciously as Tweak moved over. By now the lights had grown bigger and brighter. Tweak sat between them, rolled himself into a ball and crossed his little hedgehog claws. Just as before, the roaring came quickly and grew louder and louder, drowning out the noise of his brothers bickering over who was to get the bigger share of milky bread. Tweak squeezed his eyes tightly shut and said a little prayer to the gods of hedgehogs. The air all around him started to shake and rush again as the roaring reached its terrifying crescendo. Something warm and wet splashed all over him but Tweak stayed in his safe, trembling ball.

The roaring disappeared and Tweak slowly unfurled himself. The first thing he saw was me, sitting at the side of the road and laughing so hard that I thought my own ringpiece was going to fall off. He looked around him and saw that his two brothers who had tortured him so cruelly and for so long, were as flat as toddler tits.

Something red and stringy hung around his head and still pulsed like an angry snake. There was a huge patch of blood all over the road and Tweak was covered in it. For a moment our little legend was stunned, but then he scuttled around, dancing and laughing with delight at his bloody footprints on the tarmac.

Eventually he calmed down enough to come over to me. I clapped him on the back and got a pawful of prickles for my trouble. 'Right then, little fella,' I lit a joint and passed it to him, 'now all we've got to do is get really high and find a way of getting back at that slut of a squirrel.'

Tweak's eyes reddened and became glazed, he stood silently for a moment until I thought that he'd had a brain haemorrhage. 'Dude, I've got an idea.' He croaked. 'I reckon I know where some aidsy skag-heads left some needles…'

Bronson the Body-Building Badger

'FIFTY!' A barbarous roar rang through the trees of Gumpton Woods making all the birds flee their high perches to gossip nervously on the high winds. With a guttural growl Bronson the Badger flung away the rock that he had been bench-pressing. He sat up and snarled at his gym buddy, Samson the Beaver, who snarled in return. He got off the log that served as a bench in this most rudimentary of gyms and strutted around the clearing flexing his shoulder muscles.

'Looking good, Bronthon.' Samson lisped. Bronson didn't need to reply, he agreed.

The beaver lay down on the log and shook his arms while Bronson stood over him with the rock. 'Ready?' Bronson asked. He didn't wait for a response. He plonked the rock into Samson's out-stretched arms. Unsurprisingly it fell and smashed into the prone beaver's face.

'Ow, Bronthon. What the fuck?' Samson sat up quickly, holding his hands to his face. When he took them away, Bronson saw with no small amount of satisfaction that his lips were lacerated and one of his prominent incisors had snapped. Samson stood up and puffed out his chest. He wasn't quite as tall or broad as Bronson and they both knew that he wasn't nearly as vicious. 'You're thupposed to wait until I thay I'm ready.' He snapped.

Bronson looked down on his gym buddy with sardonic contempt. 'What are you going to do about it?' He said.

Samson licked his swollen lips and shrugged. 'Fuck it, it's only a tooth. It'll grow back in a week or two.' He looked away. 'No hard feelingth, eh?'

'None at all.' Bronson replied with a smile. 'Do you want the same stuff as last week?'

'Yeah, thothe 'roidth are great. I'm thure my chetht has bulked out more thince I've been uthing them.' Samson smiled brightly. Blood was congealing around his gum.

'I'm sure it has, too.' Bronson replied. 'I've got to go, are we still on for later?' He began to walk away without waiting for a reply.

'Yeah. Your plathe?' Samson shouted at the badger's back but Bronson made no response.

So, children, I'm going to guess that you want to know what a beaver is doing working out in our English woods? Samson was originally from Canada but when he was just a kit he was captured by some wide-eyed hippies who wanted to re-introduce a beaver population to Britain. British beavers were hunted to extinction by baldlings over five hundred years ago and lots of baldlings think it's a great idea to bring them back. I have nothing against beavers coming over here, as long as they don't take foxy jobs. Right, UKIP? The wide-eyed hippies also brought a female beaver who was sadly eaten by a homeless Romanian within weeks of being released leaving Samson a lonely migrant outcast in a foreign land. He soon realised that his inherent exoticism made him highly attractive to our native creatures and he wasted no time in capitalising upon this. With the help of his new found friend, a certain drug dealing badger by the name of Bronson, he sexually, emotionally and chemically enslaved his two ho's- Saucy Sally the Street Walking Squirrel and Bianca Bunny. Both vied for his affection and hated the other like poison. They competed ferociously, sometimes fighting tooth and claw over the next customer. Samson believed in an egalitarian approach to life and treated both with similar amounts of contempt and sugar, depending on his mood.

Bronson chuckled to himself as he walked away. Samson's chest was getting bigger alright, but not in the way that he thought. Instead of the anabolic steroids that he, Bronson was taking, he was replacing Samson's doses with the female hormone estrogen. Nasty trick, eh children? So, not only was Samson growing breasts, but his balls were also shrivelling like old balloons and he found himself weeping a lot. But why was Bronson being so nasty? The answer, children, is that Bronson was jealous. Samson had always been a ladies' beaver; exotic, articulate and debonair, whereas Bronson was an ugly, scarred brute with all the social grace of a crack-smoking gorilla. Samson selfishly kept Sally and Bianca for himself and Bronson had to pay for the privilege.

Later that evening a deep, impenetrable darkness had settled over the woods. The night was still and silent, even the owls had stayed away. A thick, immoveable blanket of cloud covered the bright heavens, but somewhere in the darkness there was noise and movement. To the passing baldling it would have sounded like the shrill squawks of nature's eternal battle of survival; to me it would have sounded like the very epitome of hell: two arguing females.

'I don't fucking care who made the most sugar for Samson today, bitch. My make-up is my make-up and you keep your thieving squirrel paws out or I will slap that smirk right off your face.' Bianca Bunny screeched.

'Now ladieth, pleath can we have one night out without a fight?' Samson's voice was pitched to reasonable in an attempt to avert the inevitable. He was summarily ignored.

'Please bitch.' Saucy Sally sucked her not inconsiderable teeth. 'The day I need to steal from a flea bitten slut-rabbit will be a sorry day indeed. I don't need to steal your shit, bitch, Samson looks after me. He buys me what I need.'

'He buys me things too, don't you Samson.' Bianca's implied threat would normally have been the point where Samson's temper broke and he would slap the pair of them, if only for some peace and quiet. But not just lately. He seemed to be becoming more cowed by the girls' constant screeching and fighting; now he just felt like crying all the time. He kept quiet. 'Beaver, you tell this bitch that she don't get no special treatment or so help me…'

'So help you what, bitch?' Saucy Sally jeered. 'What you going to do?'

'JUTHT THUT THE FUCK UP!' Samson screamed as loud as he could. The hysteria in his voice was unmistakeable. The girls exchanged a glance in the gloom. Samson's subtle shift in sensibilities of late hadn't passed unnoticed. They sank into a blessed, albeit glowering, silence.

Soon they arrived at the entrance to Bronson's sett. Samson coughed loudly until the badger appeared looking cross. 'Don't cough like that around here, baldlings might think I've got TB and send someone to shoot me.'

'Thorry Bronth.'

'It was a joke, Samson. Don't be a dickhead.' Bronson noted that the girls giggled briefly before a dark look from Samson silenced them. A fortnight ago such disrespect would have been unthinkable. The badger smiled warmly and ushered them underground.

Bronson's sett was the product of his ancestors' hard work. Each generation had burrowed a little deeper, adding extra rooms that functioned as toilets, storage rooms and bedrooms for the many cubs that were inevitable in a thriving family unit. Now though, Bronson lived alone. His parents had died long ago leaving him and his brother and sister to fend for themselves. But however much the siblings had sex, Daisy just didn't produce any cubs of her own. One day the brother was torn apart by a coach as he tried to cross the road, then not long after, during one particularly freezing winter, Bronson awoke from hibernation and feeling a little peckish decided that Daisy would do. He was never that sociable anyway and he had always found something a little repulsive about having sex with a badger. Personally, children, I can't say I blame him. But I'll try anything once though. Ha!

Bronson's inner chamber was a sparse burrow, lit by a torch that he had stolen from some baldlings he had mugged for crack. (I think we spoke about them earlier.) Bianca and Sally made themselves as comfortable as they could on the bed of moss that covered the floor.

'How's the toothy-peg, Sam?' Bronson asked, handing everyone a small off-white pill that was shaped like a heart.

'It hurth like a bathtard.'

Sally immediately leapt up and stroked Samson's face. 'I can't believe you hurt my poor baby; naughty badger.' She put the pill in her mouth and swallowed. Looking directly into Bronson's eyes, she blinked once, slowly. 'We might have to punish you tonight.'

Bronson felt a twitch and a tiny plop as his lipstick pushed its way out. 'Ooh, someone's keen.' Bianca said as she shuffled over to him. 'What do you think, Sally?'

'Oh, I think they're both keen.' Sally replied. 'Now, who's got gear?' As Samson produced a small grimy mirror and chopped out a few lines of coke, Sally positioned herself so that she had to bend over in front of Bronson to snort a line. Before she dipped her head she turned and fixed Bronson with another lingering gaze; Bianca glared at her and moved closer to the badger. Sally made a throaty growl as she inhaled her line and passed the hollow stem of grass to Bianca. She turned around in the small burrow and smiled at Bronson. 'Now, Samson,' she said as she got down on her knees without taking her eyes from Bronson's. 'I do hope we're not charging this charming badger tonight, are we?' With that she dipped her head and took Bronson's lipstick into her mouth. While he gasped and shivered, Bianca finished her line and leant over to kiss him on the mouth. Bitter flakes of cocaine were caught in her whiskers. Bronson kept his eyes open as they kissed. He watched Samson who watched him back. The hurt disdain on the beaver's tear-stained face was perfect, Bronson felt himself growing even harder in the squirrel's mouth. He smiled as he kissed Bianca, his paws roughly grabbed at her rows of nipples. Bronson closed his eyes now and stopped watching him.

35

Samson chopped out more coke. By the time he had done two lines Bronson, Sally and Bianca were one giggling mass of quivering fur. Now, children, you and I both know that Saucy Sally is carrying a certain blood-borne immunodeficiency virus, sadly for Bronson, he didn't.

*

After many hours, Bronson's little red lippy was a little redder than it was when they started. His jaw swung wildly as he bent over to do a line of coke from the heart-shaped shaved patch of skin between Saucy Sally's hind legs. As he did he saw something move in the matted hair further down beneath her tail. For a moment he thought he was hallucinating but it did it again. 'What the fuck?' Bronson muttered, just as a small worm popped his head out of Saucy Sally's little balloon knot. The worm was wearing a bandana tied around his tiny head and one eye was covered by a patch. With the other eye he tipped Bronson a wink.

'Oh, you can fuck off!' Sally exclaimed as she carefully pushed it back in with a well-manicured claw. 'Sorry, his name is Terry the Tapeworm, he helps me stay thin.' The squirrel giggled.

Suddenly Bronson felt quite sick; it had been mere minutes ago that he had been licking that very spot. He shrank backwards feeling quite disgusted. As he did his claws snagged on something on the floor behind him. 'For fuck'th thake, Bronthon, thome of uth are trying to thleep here.' Samson muttered.

'Sorry mate, I forgot you were there.' Bronson said. He peered at Saucy Sally's shaven haven, checking that the worm had gone before snorting his line.

Sally squirmed and giggled as he tickled her skin. 'I think we all forgot.'

Bianca giggled and grabbed at Bronson's flaccid cock making him jump. 'Fuck off, Bianca. Enough.' He growled.

The rabbit huffed noisily and went over to Samson who had now sat up. 'What's up Samson?' She taunted as she tried to touch his dick. 'Are you a sulky beaver tonight?'

Samson raised a paw to hit her but he seemed to think better of it at the last minute – an act of restraint that was uncharacteristic. The balance of power shifted in the low burrow.

Bianca was emboldened, her nose twitched in excitement. 'Don't think you can hit me, Samson, you over-grown American rodent. Bronson will protect me.'

Samson paused, unsure of what to do with this new situation. He moved hesitantly towards Bianca but Bronson moved between them. 'They're my bitches now, beaver. Fuck off.' He snarled.

Samson surprised everyone, including Bronson, by bursting into tears. 'Fine, fuck you all then.' The distressed beaver sobbed. 'If you think you can handle these two bitcheth then you're fucking welcome to them.' And with that he stormed out of the burrow. Bronson looked at his two prizes and shrugged his shoulders theatrically. He settled back with his forelegs crossed behind his head and a smug grin on his face. Bianca and Sally settled down with him, each snuggling into the crook of his arm. 'Yeah bitches, Bronson's the daddy now.' He said. The girls giggled and agreed. As he fell asleep Bronson thought to himself that he could get used to this life.

*

The next morning, Bronson gingerly forced open his sticky eyes, waiting for the inevitable stab of pain that he knew he deserved. The fetid air of his low burrow smelt of cigarettes and stale sex. He opened his eyes all the way now, daylight from above filtered down through the entrance tunnel providing only the dullest of grey lights. Bianca stirred next to him, her nose and whiskers twitching as she looked around, trying to establish where she was. At the same time Sally awoke too. Immediately alert she popped her head up over Bronson's chest and glared at Bianca. 'Great, I get a new daddy and *she* has to come.' She sucked her teeth and sighed heavily. 'Now, Bronson, you're going to have to get me some things from Samson's…'

Bronson's beleaguered brain attempted to process the squirrel's words. 'I…' He began but Bianca interrupted him with a piercing screech.

'Bronson. You need to sort that cunting squirrel out. If she speaks to me like that again I'm off.'

'B-but I…'

'I'm not having *her* speak to *me* like that.' Sally hopped up onto Bronson, her grey chest puffed out, her teeth bared.

'Come on then you fucking immigrant rodent, you want some of this?' Bianca jeered, beckoning with her claws.

Bronson sat up abruptly. Suddenly he was sheathed in cold sweat and trembling. 'I…I've got to go.' And he did. Quickly.

*

Bronson arrived at the gym place to find Samson pressing a log on his own. 'Alright mate…do you want some help with that?' He said rather sheepishly.

Samson finished his set of reps and threw the log away as he sat up. He glared at Bronson for a long moment until the badger was convinced that he was going to tell him to fuck off. Finally he spoke. 'I take it they're arguing.'

Bronson nodded. 'Like you wouldn't believe.'

'Oh, I believe it alright. That-th my life…' Samson looked sad and sorry for himself.

'Right…' Bronson looked around him uncomfortably. 'Look, mate, I've been giving you the wrong pills. I gave you female hormones.'

Samson laughed. 'That explainth a lot. You're a cock Bronthon. You owe me a lot of coke for that one.'

Bronson smiled a genuine, warm smile. 'You've got a deal, as long as you clear those fucking bitches out of my burrow!'

Clarence the Nosy Crow

Sometimes in baldling neighbourhoods you get that one house where the curtains always seem a bit twitchy. As you wander by you might detect the smallest flutter of movement as lacy nets fall back into place, or the darkness in an unlit room seems to shift ever so slightly. These are the people who always seem to know what is happening on the street; who is out of work again, whose car tax still hasn't been renewed and who is fucking who. These reptiles are rewarded for their snoopery by the Filth in the form of yellow and black stickers that go in their window proclaiming 'this is a neighbourhood watch area.' In Gumpton Woods we have our own nosy cunt – his name is Clarence and he's a crow.

My enmity with the corvine cock sucker is a grudge nearly as deep and old as a Middle Eastern land feud. Once upon a time, when your friend Frankie was nowt more than a wide-eyed kit, Clarence committed the lowest of sins – he grassed me up to Old Ma Francesca for smoking the herb. Francesca Fox was a formidable

42

vixen, a fox not to be fucked with. Clarence had sniffed me out as he was flying over and he wasted no time in fluttering down to the old burrow to tell her what he'd smelt. Old Ma Francesca was furious, she beat me so hard that half my tail died and dropped off leaving me with the rakish stump I am left with today. I never held it against the old girl. Ok, so I ate the next litter that came along after me and I shagged my sister but none of that was out of spite; a fox has got to do what a fox has got to do. But from that moment on, the crow and I were sworn enemies.

After Old Ma Francesca had left for greener pastures I became don of the den, ruler of the roost; apex predator in this heaven forsaken green blight. When I walked through the woods the bushes would tremble and shake as tiny creatures rushed to get out of my path. Birds would take to the wing and even those meat-head bodybuilders, Samson and Bronson, were wary of me. The woods lived under the thrall of my vulpine mystique; all creatures acquiesced to my superior power. All except that bastard crow. Every time I stopped somewhere to skin up, Clarence would sweep down from the trees, flying at me, making me spill my joint. 'CAW,

FRANKIE'S ON THE WEED AGAIN. CAW, THE FOX IS

GETTING STONED. CAW, CAW.' Cunt.

'What's the problem Frankie, we thought you were the man?'

I hear you ask. Well, children, you're right, I am, but I like a bit of

peace and quiet to toke a little jay and that bastard bird wouldn't

give me a moment's peace. But that wasn't the main problem. When

all the animals in Gumpton Woods knew that I'd been smoking

again they'd take the piss and start running around like they were

Billy Big Balls because they thought that I was too stoned to catch

them. Obviously I'd rip their fucking heads off and shit in their

necks, just to prove a point...well I would do if I wasn't too stoned

to catch them. The thing is, children, being an aficionado of the herb

of love doesn't exactly lend itself to being the daddy in these woods.

I needed to cultivate an image of cold, brutish violence; not come

across as some hippy fox that weaves daisies in his fur and reads The

Big Issue. I needed to teach the crow a lesson, and I needed

everyone to see what happens when you fuck with Frankie.

A smart fox knows that opportunity can come knocking at

any time. My chance to get even with Clarence came one grumpy, grey day when far off thunder rumbled ominously, portending the coming storm. I had spent a rewarding day lying in some long grass, smoking and contemplating the bad-tempered movement of the clouds. I heard the distinct cawing sound of a crow and rolled my eyes expecting Clarence to dive bomb me and shatter my peace, but no attack came. I poked my head over the grass and saw a black crow with its back to me. It was just a little smaller than Clarence, I quickly realised that it must be Mrs Clarence. Suddenly a plan was born. They call us foxes cunning for a reason.

While Mrs Clarence and I were getting acquainted, Clarence was circling the woods looking for a meal. He dipped and soared on the high winds scanning the ground below until he saw what he was looking for – a tasty bit of carrion left on the floor of woods. He dived, screeching his excitement like a fat kid in McDonalds. Was it some of Frankie's leftovers? Or even Bronson's? Who knew, who cared? In Gumpton Woods a meal is a meal, eat first, ask later. Clarence landed and checked around, making sure that the provider of this fine feast wasn't poised to catch himself some fresh birdie. Little did he know that I was behind a tree, watching and waiting.

Some foxes have tricks up their proverbial sleeves; I was wearing mine on my hand.

The fresh corpse was unrecognisable, whatever had done a number on this poor bugger had certainly done a good number. The creature had been all but turned inside out. A sticky ribcage protruded from the still-warm mass of red, stringy flesh and spilled blood. The head was gone; maybe it had been removed as part of some cunning plan? Clarence wasn't clever enough to notice. He tucked in, pulling the delicious entrails out of its cavity and pecking away with greedy gusto. I like to think that he wondered if he should take some back to Mrs Clarence who was back at the nest keeping their eggs nice and warm.

I waited until Clarence was bespattered in gore and full to burping. I stepped quietly from behind a tree. Clarence paid me no attention as he picked and pecked and pulled and crunched. I held out my new glove, my paws made me a clumsy puppeteer but by playing with various tendons I managed to control Mrs Clarence's beak. 'Oh, Clarence. How is your meal? I do hope you've saved some for me!' I said in my best falsetto voice, trying not to laugh.

Clarence looked up, tensed to take flight. His beak dropped open and a small, purple tatter of gristle fell out. 'No, you haven't...' He said in a small voice. He looked down at his meal and the penny dropped. 'CAW, FRANKIE, YOU WANKER! CAW, CAW.' He flew at my head, taking me quite by surprise. I hadn't quite expected such a violent reaction, I mean, we're animals, not baldlings; a short and meaningless life is expected in our world and it is all the fairer for it. In a place where everything eats everything else and you are but a meal postponed, death is accepted, nay, *expected*. In the baldling world you have managed to separate yourselves from the laws of the wild, you're an apex predator who's revolted by murder. It's a bit like being a dick-fearing prostitute. This is why I was so shocked at Clarence's reaction. Ok, so I'd murdered and eviscerated the love of his life and mother of his eggs and then I made him eat her, but come on; where was his sense of humour?

The crow flew at me like never before, pecking, squawking, biting. I had to run for the burrow, laughing all the way. The crow harried my retreat until he gave up, presumably to go and tell the eggs that Mummy would be shit onto the bonnet of a Ford Mondeo in three to five hours. When I got there, Tweak was sitting in my favourite corner with his feet up and his snuffly little nose in my ganja pot. I thought about cuffing him around the head but he passed me a splif so I forgave him. Mrs Frankie was nowhere to be seen, thank the gods. She'd been questioning my relationship with the hedgehog and making hints that I needed to assert my foxiness around the woods a little more. It really wouldn't do for her to see me get chased by a crow and let Tweak steal my weed!

'What are you looking so harassed for, Frankie?' Tweak said with a dopey grin on his face.

I grinned back. 'I just put Clarence straight.' I went on to tell Tweak the whole story, puffing my chest out with pride as I got to the sticky bits.

'Wow…that's pretty dark.' Tweak said when I'd finished. 'Aren't you worried that he'll try and get his own back on you?'

'What's a crow going to do to a fox?' I scoffed at Tweak's wide-eyed innocence.

'I don't know…crows can be pretty evil when they want to be. They say you should never cross a crow.' The daft hedgehog actually looked worried.

I stared at him a moment, trying to work out if he was having me on. That simple pin-cushion looked too stoned to be lying. 'Fuck off, Tweak. I'm the daddy around here, not Clarence.'

'Honest man, he might do some voodoo crow stuff on you. You'd better watch out.'

'And you'd better *get* out before Mrs Frankie gets home and accuses you of bringing ticks into the burrow.' I said laughing.

Tweak managed to puff up his chest and look all indignant. 'I'll have you know hedgehogs are the cleanest creatures in the forest, Frankie Foulbowel.'

Just then Mrs Frankie walked into the burrow. 'Hey Frankie. Oh…hi Tweak…' She threw me that 'why is *he* here' look. I decided that now would be a good time to point out that I had owned the crow and so I told her the story.

Mrs Frankie sucked her teeth like a builder who's been asked when he'll finish. 'Oh Frankie, you've fucked up there.'

'See.' Tweak said smugly.

'Shut up, Tweak.' Mrs Frankie and I replied in unison.

'Messing with crows is bad news,' Mrs Frankie continued. 'I thought that was why you never retaliated when he hassled you.'

'That's because he's always too stoned.' Tweak piped up helpfully.

Mrs Frankie smiled. 'I could warm to the hedgehog as long as he's not got ticks.' Tweak went to speak but thought better of it. She went on. (She does that.) 'My dad once told me that his Uncle Eddie killed a crow and the very next day he was caught by dogs and torn apart.'

'Your dad's Uncle Eddie told me that story too. He was a pathological liar.'

'That's not the point. Crows are evil and you're going to die a nasty death tomorrow.' Sniffed Mrs Frankie.

'Well in that case I'm going to get as stoned as a mother fucker tonight!' I cackled. Clearly I'd won the point because she turned her back on me. With that, Tweak and I left.

*

Later on, after half a dozen too many doobie snacks, Tweak and I were sat in the gnarled thicket of Rhododendrons that was left over from when Gumpton Woods was an ornamental park on some rich bloke's estate. 'What's that, Frankie? I hear you ask. Gumpton Woods was someone's garden?' Yes, children, it most certainly was. The first earl of Gumpton was also the last. He was a petty crook by the name of Tommy Shanksworth who turned over the most profitable brothel in Cheapside, sometime around 1690. The story goes that he kitted himself out in new robes and went to a ball where he managed to pull Mary II while her husband, William of Orange, was overseas kicking someone's arse. Shanksworth turned out to be so skilled with the tongue that Mary showered him with gifts including the estate of Gumpton and an earldom of the same name. Of course, William of Orange returned from oppressing someone and had a hot sword shoved so far up young Tommy's jacksie that he tasted steel before he died.

Buried deep in the rhododendrons, Tweak and I were unassailable. At the centre of the thicket was a cracked old sundial that was wreathed with generations of living and dead ivy. Tweak and I sat smoking with our backs against this monument to baldling culture, enjoying the symphony of the woods as darkness fell. That time of day always feels like a changing of the guard to me. The sedate twittering of the birds falls silent voice by voice, to be replaced by the harsh twoos and caas of owls and the blundering crash of Bronson as he wakes and barrels through the undergrowth looking for dinner, a fix and a fuck; in whichever order he can get them.

'Here, Frank. Sally gave me these.' Tweak grunted.

'Remember what happened the last time Sally gave you something to take?'

'Nuh man. These are mushrooms; nice and mellow. I took a few earlier.' Tweak replied. Suddenly his voice sounded full of stars. I needed some of that if I were to die a horrible death on the morrow.

'Give them here you spiny little bastard.' I said, holding out a paw. Tweak put a big bag of mushrooms in it and I promptly tipped them into my mouth.

'Frankie you prick, they were supposed to last us both all night. You did too much man, too much. They're gonna fuck you up.' The concern in Tweak's voice was more frightening than his words. What had I done? A cold sweat crept under my fur, puckering my skin like an old man's ball bag.

'I'm Frankie Foulbowel, I can handle it.' I said with a cavalier confidence that I didn't feel.

We sat and smoked some more. The moon peeped through the trees, riding high and bright, seeming to bathe the woods in cold silver. I shivered, a long slow shudder that started in the back of my head and slid down my spine, caressing each vertebrae with a delicious chill. A grin spread across my face. I yawned, tensing every muscle in my body. I slowly exhaled feeling my flesh fall away from my bones. A breeze made the branches of the trees click and clatter together like a battle of wooden soldiers. Each star in the sky left a tiny wake, light-years long, as it passed through the inky ocean. I looked back down to earth and found that Tweak was watching me with a maternal smile. 'Are you coming up, Frankie? Is that nice?' He said. His face looked so soft, I wanted to rub it against my cold wet nose. Or my cold wet nose against it? I wasn't sure but… 'Frankie! What the hell are you doing?' Ah, I realised that I was doing just that. Tweak looked alarmed.

'Let's go for a walk. The night is so beautiful.' I bounded to my feet, suddenly infused with an electric curiosity that made my head crackle and buzz.

'I'm really not sure we should, dude. You're pretty wasted…' Tweak started to reply but it too late, I was gone.

The floor of the woods felt like a thick carpet under my paws. My tail swayed gently as it brushed through wet leaves leaving an imperceptible groove, a signature of my passing through.

The dark canopy above swayed gently, diffusing silver light into the myriad flakes of a disco ball. Tweak shuffled as fast as he could to keep up but he was soon gone, forgotten like each thought that passed through my mind, killed by the anticipation of those to follow. Each twig that cracked underpaw, every leaf that whispered as it passed me by: these were the medium in which my tale was written, the letters and words which told my story. The light died slowly, strangled by a blackened cloud, theatrically stretching out its inevitable demise as the woods plunged into an inky darkness. I looked over my shoulder, where the hell was Tweak?

I heard something in the trees above. I turned my head, instinctively curious. High above me a small part of the night moved, a spot of blackness settled on a branch. My heart froze, stammering over a beat before finding the next. It was him. It was the devil. I fancied I could see the cold jewels of his eyes watching me, calculating that I was alone, I was vulnerable; I was battered. I stood rooted to the spot. A small trickle of Frankie fluid dampened the ground beneath me. I had no defence, claws and teeth were forgotten. Fighting was something that others could do but was beyond the reach of this poor, drug-adled creature. The blackness fell, swooping from the tree with an ear-rending CAAAAW. The spell was broken, I ran. The crow pecked at my head, piercing flesh, plucking chunks of fur. I tried to turn, to say something, to blub that I was sorry. Every time I saw him his eyes burned into me with a malevolent fury that made me weep like a kit. He swooped again and again, too many times to count. Pecking, snapping, screeching evil. My breath was tearing my throat, my legs turned to jelly. Panicked, I dived under a scratchy holly bush and waited for the end. The crow shook the bush, cawing and screaming like an avian banshee until finally he let up, leaving me to the tender mercy of the night.

I stayed under the bush, too scared to leave. The horrible mushrooms worked their way through my brain bringing hallucinations and shivering nightmares that left me drenched in freezing sweat. Eventually grey light and sanity crept back into the world. Mrs Frankie found me, still cowering under a holly bush. I was covered in cuts and peck marks; bloodied, bruised and bashed. She didn't pass judgement or make any snidey comments. She managed to help me back to the burrow before any of the other animals saw me. My pride was hurt but my reputation was intact. By now my terror had abated; now I was angry. Angry? I was fucking furious. I was going to get even with Clarence the Crow if it was the last thing I ever did.

Touché the Turtoise

Our next tale begins one magical springtime morning when the woods felt revived and fresh. The trees were showing the bright green shoots of this year's growth; Bianca Bunny's latest litter of cross-eyed incestlings were peeping curiously from the entrance to their warren; and deep under the tannin stained waters of Petticoat Pond, Skibadee the Turtle had the twitch. She flapped a graceful flipper stirring up an eon of sediment, as she sighed and tried to position herself to make it easier for Touché – her partner by default and the only chance she possibly had of getting shagged. Sadly it was no good; Touché huffed and puffed but Skibadee was three times his size and he lacked the imagination to do much more than rub his sticky bits all over the back of her shell. That doesn't sound very satisfying, does it children? Poor Skibadee!

It wasn't that spring was the only time when Touché tried it on, far from it! The randy little turtle spent half his life trying to mount his mate, however, spring was the only time of year when

Skibadee had any interest whatsoever. As Touche was too stupid and ill-equipped to make anything happen, Skibadee's sighs of frustration could be heard all around the pond.

The reason why Touché was so thick ties in very closely to why there were two American turtles in an English pond in the first place. You see, Samson wasn't the only foreign species in our fair woods. A long time ago someone made a cartoon about ninja turtles in order to manipulate parents into buying lumps of plastic for their spoilt offspring. Now, there is one certain type of baldling who is slightly more evil than the others. Pet shop owners. These slave-traders sell poor, incarcerated animals to serve and entertain other baldlings. If I ever come across one, children, I'm going to fuck his eye-socket. However, I digress. These slave-traders realised that they could make a quick quid out of this craze for turtles so they imported lots of wild ones from America. They were kept in tiny containers as they crossed the Atlantic and lots of them died on the way. It was a terrible business, children. When these spoilt little brats got the turtles home they found out, much to their half-witted disappointment, that they didn't eat pizza, do martial arts or speak like stoned Californian surfers. It didn't take long before the spoilt brats got bored and moved on to the next ridiculous consumption fad and the poor turtles ended up flushed away or released into the wild. Remember kids, pets are for life, not just for the duration of your E-number shortened attention spans.

A little boy called Matty was one such lad. Although his attention span was as shrivelled as the rest, he had a kind heart buried somewhere beneath several pounds of subcutaneous lard. He released his two little turtles in Petticoat Pond in Gumpton Woods. Over time these two turtles had a girl and boy who grew up and had a girl and boy who, by chance, had a boy and a girl who had Skibadee and Touché. When there's a gene-pool this shallow, nature has a habit of pointing out that this isn't the way it's done. For a baldling reference point you might try looking at Iceland or any small town in Wales. Skibadee grew up to be quite normal but poor little Touché scraped the bottom of this particular genetic barrel and turned out to be a little bit simple.

Now children, let me point out that there is nothing wrong with being stupid, some stupid people can be very successful; look at

60

footballers, glamour models and local politicians. Touché's major problem was that he was too stupid to learn to swim, which as an aquatic animal put him at quite a disadvantage. Somehow he managed to scrape through his life by living on the shit that sinks to the bottom of the pond and scrambling up the banks to breathe every now and then. Having no natural predators due to their ethnic minority status meant that even though he was almost entirely immobile he survived. However, when Touché went on land something miraculous happened; he could not only move, the little bastard was like greased lightning! He loved being on solid ground and even Skibadee had to say that when she saw him flying across the forest floor she felt a fluttering in her fallopian flower! But the joy of movement was only ever short-lived, for Touché was a creature of the water, sooner or later he had to return, otherwise he would quickly fall foul of the kind of skin herpes usually reserved for children with sensitivity to non-biological washing powder, and that wasn't very sexy at all. What were those poor turtles to do!

So on this charming spring day when the woods were full of joyful beings waking up to an exciting new year of hope and opportunity, Skibadee was frustrated and Touché was emasculated. Skibadee glided gracefully through the water to rest in the sunshine on her favourite log and our Touché and his swollen bollocks sank like several funny sized stones to the bottom of the pond to sulk and eat shit.

Skibadee sighed a great big sigh just as Saucy Sally was scampering by. 'Hey, Skibs. What's up with you?' Sally shouted from the bank of the pond.

With another depressed sigh, Skibadee hauled herself off the log and belly flopped into the water. She flapped over to where Sally waited for her and climbed slowly out onto the bank. 'Hi Sally. It's Touché…'

Sally nodded sympathetically. 'It's twitch time again, yeah? Poor Skibadee, I take it he still hasn't learnt how to fuck you properly?'

'No. I doubt he ever will.' Skibadee sighed again.

'Well I could suggest cross-species sex.' Sally said brightly. 'It's not going to produce many turtle eggs but a good stiff cock is a good stiff cock at the end of the day!' Skibadee looked at her with barely disguised revulsion. 'Don't judge, a girl has to make her money somehow.' Sally sniffed loftily. 'If he's no good at being a turtle why don't you get him made into a tortoise, everyone knows that they've got massive cocks.'

'How would you know?' Skibadee asked, her eyes wide with shock.

'How do you think?' Sally replied, tipping her a lubricious wink. 'Take him to Mikhail the Mole, he does dodgy back-street species change operations. Then see how snobby you want to be about taking a bit of strange cock. Anyway, I've got to go. I've got a midday appointment with Bronson and if I'm late he'll beat me harder than he will anyway. Laters.' With that Sally turned on her hind paws, flashed her vendible tale and scampered up the nearest tree.

Skibadee flopped back into the pond and flapped around aimlessly for a while. Sally could be right, maybe if Touché underwent species-reassignment surgery then he would finally be able to give her the scaly length that she so wanted and needed. She swan to the bottom of the pond and began to look for Touché so she could tell him the good news.

*

As the sun came up the next day, Skibadee and Touché wandered from the river bank looking for the tell-tale signs of Mikhail the Mole. They set out so early because Mikhail was a nocturnal creature who spent his nights foraging underground and performing brutal surgery on anyone who could pay him. Mikhail had gained his surgery skills in the Russian *bratva* where he was an interrogator charged with carving up rival gang members until they looked like dolls in order to make them talk. After many years of hacking off deformed ears and noses that had been broken more times than a politician's promise, Mikhail had decided that it was time to leave Moscow and head to a calmer, more serene place to retire. He needed money to spend on his addictive fetish for drinking cough mixture and having Saucy Sally 'turn his lights out' by throttling him with a used johnny while she blew crack smoke up his arse and wanked him off into a pair of children's knickers that he'd found wrapped around some old bones deep underground. Obviously sex of such kinky specificity came at a premium and that grabbing squirrel ho-bag fleeced him for every penny that she could. So he had decided to dust off his old surgery tools and make the animals of Gumpton Woods feel more complete and like 'themselves' by hacking bits off them and re-arranging what was left. He gave Bronson a wider neck, he gave Sally a nip and tuck to make her special squirrel place a bit tighter and he gave yours truly a cock extension that had Mrs Frankie weeping into her pillow for a month.

Before the two wandering turtles had gone too far into the woods they came across a small mound of fresh mud that was pushed up between two tree roots. They exchanged a hopeful glance and began sniffing around, trying to dig into the dirt. Soon the ground beneath them trembled and a small, twitching, fleshy bud, not unlike an old lady's clitoris, pushed its way up through the ground. It was followed by a small, black, scarred creature that scowled at them with sightless eyes. 'What the fuck do you want?' He said in a thick Russian accent, his pink little nose twitching as he smelt the air. 'You taste like two little turtles. Tell me your business, little turtles. It is nearly Mikhail bedtime.'

'Hi Mikhail.' Skibadee said nervously. 'We've come to see if you could make my Touché into a tortoise because he makes a shit turtle.'

'Hm… this is not very expensive operation. Essentially tortoise is just sun-proof turtle, all we need do is apply sun-cream and cut off nose, then break feet and reform into more tortoise shape. I do tomorrow. Cost you two hundred pounds.' Mikhail replied. He yawned and stretched his arms.

'But, Mr Mikhail, I'm afraid that we don't have that kind of money. Is there any other way that we could pay you?'

Mikhail shrugged his shoulders angrily. 'You make egg? I sell turtle egg to some mental Nicaraguan man who can't make the hump-hump no more. He think they good aphrodisiac; I make money. You make two before bandages come off or I come and take shell.'

'But he needs his shell.' Skibadee said with more than a little alarm. 'Without it he'll die.'

'Meh.' Said Touché. Which, unfortunately, was all he was capable of.

Mikhail shrugged. 'Is risk but if no risk, no tortoise. Understand?'

Skibadee nodded gravely. It was a risk but it was one she was willing to take. 'Ok then, Mr Mikhail, we'll be back at the same time tomorrow.'

'Meh.' Said Touché.

*

The next morning Skibadee and Touché waddled back to the mound where they had found Mikhail the day before. Mikhail was waiting for them and smoking an acrid joint that made Skibadee's eyes hurt. 'Mr Mikhail, whatever is in that splif? It's making my throat burn!' She said coughing and spluttering.

'Just little angel dust. It help me not shake when I operation.'

'Ah, I see.' Replied Skibadee. 'Doesn't that make you feel better, Touché? See, I told you he's a professional.'

'Meh.' Said Touché.

They followed Mikhail deep down into his labyrinthine tunnels until they reached a small chamber. 'Here is where I operation.' Mikhail said in the inky darkness.

'But don't you need light to operate?' Skibadee asked.

'I am mole, I am blind. I operation by feel. Not to worry, turtle is safe in my hands.' A disjointed laugh echoed around the hole.

'Oh.' Said Skibadee.

'Meh.' Said Touché.

And so in the thick darkness Mikhail did his work while Skibadee wandered back to the surface for a bit of fresh air. Eventually the little turtle waddled to the edge of Mikhail's hole. He flopped out into the daylight, squinting in the early morning sunshine. He had little bandages covering all four of his flippers (or were they now feet?), his pained eyes peered over the bandages that covered what was left of his snout and his skin was covered in a thick white goo that made him look like he had been the special guest of honour at a Japanese bukkake party.

'How are you, Touché?' Asked Skibadee. 'Does it hurt?'

In a very small, very unhappy voice, Touché said: 'Meh.'

Skibadee led him back to the pond, fretting and worrying the whole way. She moved twigs out of his path to make the journey easier and for a while she even let him climb upon her back for a ride. When they got to the pond Skibadee climbed into the water but Touché waited at the side; it took Skibadee a moment to realise that he couldn't go in the water anymore, he was now a tortoise!

Over the coming days and weeks spring advanced, as is its wont. The snowdrops gave way to the daffodils then the bluebells and used condom packets began to appear again at the carpark where the doggers and dog walkers would sometimes meet. With every passing day Touché became more used to being an animal of the land. He learned to make himself a burrow, hunt for grubs and generally do all the things that land animals do. Skibadee, meanwhile, got more and more lonely in the pond with no-one for company but a waterboatman whom nobody liked. Touché's little feet got better and better until finally Mikhail said that his bandages were ready to come off.

A grand unveiling was called and some of the animals of the woods got together to see Touché's new look. Most of the crew were there. Samson sat with Sally and Bianca either side of him, both tried to sit on his lap so he had to slap them and tell them to cut it out; Bronson stood at the back flexing his muscles and twitching a bit; Tweak and my good self were skinning up while that Catholic cunt Gerry looked on in disgust. Clarence sat in a tree, watching for Tweak and I to pass the joint so that he could make a fuss. After my messed up night on the mushrooms I had laid low for a while. It took some time to lick my wounds, both physical and psychological. I needed many a splif with Tweak and an awful lot of Mrs Frankie applying the lipstick, if you know what I mean. But eventually I grew strong enough and brave enough to face the world again.

Clarence had a smug "I've-got-one-up-on-you-Frankie" look on his face. I didn't mind, revenge comes to the patient.

Mikhail made Touché sit on an old tree stump holding a placard that said 'MIKHAIL THE MOLE'S HANDIWORK.' Everyone, including yours truly, was excited to see what he had done, but no-one was more excited than Skibadee. In the weeks that had passed her hankering for turtle cock had grown to a suffocating fever until she could barely sleep at night for the thought of finally receiving the length that she truly deserved. Mikhail the Mole cleared his throat importantly and strutted around in front of the tree with his fleshy little nose twitching like Skibadee's fleshy little rose. 'Now see here, animal of Gumpton Woods. Here is new resident, I give you…Touché the Tortoise!' With a flourish he jumped up onto the stump and ripped off Touché's bandages revealing the handsome, chiselled face of a very sexy tortoise. Skibadee's heart was all a-flutter and she blushed her appreciation. 'Do not forget, Turtle lady, you owe two turtle eggs.' Mikhail held out his mole claw expectantly. At this point I decided to weigh in, in my own inimitable way.

'Hang on, Mikhail. Didn't you do the surgery so that Skibadee could get laid?' I said.

'This is true Mr Foulbowel. I believe I did operation to help you with problem too. I remember your cock, it was pigeon's toe.'

'Alright Mikhail, hush now.' I said, a little embarrassed. Tweak had the nerve to snigger so I cuffed him round the back of the head and got a fucking splinter for my trouble. But I was not to be deterred. 'So, if Touché's bandages are only just coming off, how is she supposed to give you two eggs straight away? Give them a week to get their jiggy on.'

Mikhail started to protest but he was shouted down by all the other animals. Eventually he stormed away muttering to himself in Russian. Everyone cheered but we all knew that Skibadee had better pay up soon or Mikhail would start chopping.

The crowd went back to their lives because, to be quite frank, a turtle's sex life just isn't that fascinating, unless your name is David Attenborough in which case it's probably worth a wank. Skibadee eyed Touché with longing; Touché reciprocated. She waddled her fat arse over to him as he clambered down from the tree stump. She sat in the dirt and waited for him to mount her. And he tried…bless him. But he was still just too small! They tried different positions for what seemed like hours. All the while Tweak and I, caned as a dominatrix's man-slave, watched from behind a tree, laughing our fucking arses off! Eventually Skibadee threw her claws into the air in exasperation. 'Touché, I'm afraid that although Mikhail has made you look like a tortoise you're still just a turtle with a tiny cock!'

What were they to do? They still had Mikhail's debt to pay, otherwise Touché's shell was as good as gone. But they had no chance of making an egg and Touché was stuck as a tortoise, but not even a proper tortoise – a turtoise!

As Touché sulked back to his burrow and Skibadee slid gracefully into the murky pond, Tweak and I slowly regained the ability to breathe and talk. 'Do you know what, Frankie?' Tweak managed to say between receding giggles. 'I kind of feel bad for laughing at those two. Shall we try and help?'

73

'I was just thinking the same thing, my spiny friend.' I replied. And I was, I'm nice like that. 'I've got just the idea. Come on, let's go tree climbing!'

A sly glint appeared in Tweak's eye. 'Are you thinking what I'm thinking?'

'Yep.' I said triumphantly. 'We're going to get our own back on that fucking crow.'

As we saw earlier, children, our hedgehog friend isn't the most graceful of creatures and so your Uncle Frankie found himself shining up a large elm tree, muttering like a pre-menstrual Mutley. Now, you may have noticed that you don't generally see too many tree climbing foxes. The reason for this is that tree climbing is a mug's game, but Saucy Sally does nothing for free and I wasn't about to pay her good money to do anything other than lick my balloon knot, so I had to climb myself.

I snuck as quietly as only the sneakiest of foxes can, slithering from branch to branch like a vulpine ninja. When I got near to the top I saw what I was looking for – Clarence the crow's nest. Clarence was there, sitting on four shiny little eggs, still weeping over the sad loss of Mrs Clarence. Those eggs probably weren't even his but that mug was warming them with his little arse anyway. They were his pride and joy, the next generation of baby birds. I sat waiting as it got dark but that gobby little bastard wouldn't go anywhere. I was just starting to think that he was settled for the night and that I was either going to have to climb down and try again tomorrow, or spend the night sitting in a bloody tree. But Clarence poked his head out, had a look around and then flew away, doubtless to make one last sweep of the neighbourhood. Nosy cunt. I executed a death defying leap over to the nest and found four little green eggs, sat on a soft white bed of cotton that Clarence had stolen from a feminine hygiene bin. I almost had a moment of conscience as I thought about poor Mrs Clarence and her final legacy to the world, but then I remembered that I'm Frankie Fucking Foulbowel the Famous Philandering Fox, I stole those eggs and scarpered down that tree before the crow could come back.

The very next morning Tweak and I sauntered up to the pond. While we sat smoking a doobie and throwing in small stones,

Touché came to join us and Skibabdee came to the surface to see what was going on. 'Morning Skibs,' I said. 'We've got you a present.' I held out the four eggs in my paws while she swam over to see.

'Thank you so much Mr Foulbowel. But won't Mikhail realise that they aren't turtle eggs?'

'Nah. He's blind, he won't know a thing.'

'But isn't it a bit naughty to rip off the disabled?' Skibadee replied.

'Not if you stand to profit, just ask the Department of Work and Pensions.' I said with a wink.

'I can't thank you enough, Mr Foulbowel. Now we can pay off that grabbing Russian mole and get him to change Touché back into a turtle. He might be a shit turtle but he's my shit turtle.' Skibadee turned to her lover and placed an affectionate claw on his deformed one.

'Meh.' Said Touché.

And so Touché and Skibadee lived unhappily ever after in a state of perpetual sexual dissatisfaction, just like so many baldling couples. Mikhail was happy enough, he got the eggs he was owed and more to reverse the operation. Unfortunately the Nicaraguan man tried to take them and one of them hatched in his throat choking him to death. The word is that Mikhail was pretty annoyed with me but as the guy was dead and couldn't ask for a refund I think I got away with it. The only problem was Clarence.

The Fearsome Threesome

A long, long time ago there was a baldling who said that for every action there is an equal and opposite reaction. By stealing Clarence's precious eggs, by participating in Tweak's AIDS giving revenge, by mugging off Mikhail with iffy eggs; I had provided a series of actions; those I had wronged were to provide the reaction. The sad thing is, children, that some animals don't know their place and won't learn it by gentle lessons.

In the darkest depths of the darkest night a clandestine meeting took place under an old hollow tree. Mikhail the Mole, Saucy Sally and Clarence the Crow eyed one another suspiciously in the gloom. As the instigator of this iniquitous infamy, Mikhail opened the meeting. 'Now then, Squirrel, Crow. We three have common problem that needs solved, do we not? A certain fox by name of Frankie has fucked with us all. Crow, he fed you wife, Squirrel, fox gave you the AIDS. He cheat Mikhail with fake eggles to make Mikhail look fool. We all have scores to settle.'

'I sorted that bastard fox out before and I'll do it again. We just have to catch him when he's pickled.' Clarence said. I didn't witness this but I can imagine that the smug cunt was grinning like a politician on payday.

'Fool of a crow.' Mikhail sneered. 'Fox is tougher than you give credit. He will crush you for humiliating him.'

'Mikhail's right.' Saucy Sally said. 'We need to fix the fox forever.'

'How are we going to do that? In case neither of you has noticed, he's the predator around here. We can hardly hunt him.' Clarence squaked.

'No, we can't.' Said Mikhail, with sly glint in his stupid, pointless, non-functioning eyes. 'But there are those who can.'

'Surely you don't mean fox-hunting, do you? That was banned by the baldlings.' Sally said.

'I have contact, rich Chelseaite who didn't make it on to show. He buy his nose candy from same man as me. He say that he have rich friends who angry that they no hunt the fox no more. I say to him "Come to Gumpton, I have the fox who needs to be catch." But I need little help. Foulbowel is tricksy fox, we all know. He need luring into open, and then.' Mikhail slowly drew a finger across his throat in the universal mime of murder.

This would be an appropriate point for you to ask, "so how come you know all this Frankie?" Well, children, it just so happened that my favourite chuffing chum was foraging behind the rotten tree when the treasonous trio arrived. Being a nosy hedgehog, he hung around to see what gossip he could pick up, nothing could prepare him for the dastardliness that was unfolding. He waited while that sneaky talpid outlined his plan, then he came straight round to mine where Mrs Frankie was smoking the cigar. When I heard what was going on, I made her stop straight away; this was more important, this was war. Mrs Frankie and Tweak listened with wide eyes as I outlined my counter plan.

*

I had to carry on as normal, it was imperative that Mikhail and his new friends didn't suspect anything. Clarence would appear from time to time, crowing about the herb and hassling me about his eggs. He would fly high above me and then swoop down, aiming at my head. I was always careful to react with my normal savagery. All the while I kept an eye out for the sign that judgement day was coming. Each time I leapt at the crow, each time I saw Saucy Sally scampering along a branch, pretending not to give me sidelong glares and a smug, knowing smile, each time I saw one of Mikhail's piles of spoil, I chuckled inside.

The days flitted by as they do and I started to wonder if the grand plan to serve me my cold dish of just deserts had been abandoned; had all my preparations been in vain? I desperately hoped not, I really had excelled myself this time. Then one day a breathless Tweak arrived at my door.

I had tasked Tweak with employing spies – knowledge would be the key to winning this battle. So it was that one day while Tweak was resting from his night-time exertions in his lair under the oak tree, one of his minions appeared. A moth by the name of

Michael Mothins flew in and fluttered around Tweak's head, tickling his nose until he sneezed himself awake.

'Wha...whathefuckisthatshit...fucking...oh, hi Michael.' Tweak mumbled, rubbing the sleepy dust from his eyes. 'What is it?'

'Mikhail's...had a meeting with...Clarence and Sally... It's happening now...they're coming for Frankie!' Michael gasped. As I understand it, it's pretty difficult to hover and talk at the same time.

'Good work, Michael Mothins. Frankie and I will remember you well for this.' Tweak replied, sounding a little like a mafioso gangster.

'Do you...promise that you won't eat my next...litter of grubs, Tweak? You...did promise me.'

Tweak grinned. 'I'll see what I can do.' Michael flew away with a distinct sense that he had just been done. And he had, but no one cares what insects think.

Tweak hurried to den and burst in with an unhinged glint in his eye. 'It's happening, Frankie.' He squeaked with barely contained glee. 'It's happening now.' As if to punctuate my hedgehog friend's statement, from far away near the edge of Gumpton Woods a hunting bugle sounded and the dogs bayed a blood curdling reply.

Not one of us knows how he will feel as he awaits the battle. Some will tremble with fear, their bowels and bladders weakening as the distant rumble of violent thunder approaches inch by inexorable inch. Others will feel an immeasurable sadness at the potential for having to leave this wonderful life earlier than they had intended. Me? I sharpened my fucking claws as I skipped towards my rendezvous with the timekeeper. The distant storm had reached full ear-shot now. Thunder had become the relentless battering of shod hooves on the woodland floor. The dogs barked, leading the hunt, their sharp, excited yelps told me that they'd already found my scent. These barbarous echoes seemed to resonate through the years from the dark time when rich people thought that it was entirely appropriate to chase frightened, defenceless foxes through field and forest before savagely eviscerating their trampled corpse. As I sauntered through my Gumpton Woods, friend and prey came out to watch me pass. I kept my chin and my stump of a tail held high. Old

Ma Francesca raised me to be the prince of the forest and if I was to do battle with the forces of evil it would be with pride.

I reached the clearing. The hunt was close enough now that I could feel the ground tremble. I looked up in the trees, sniffing the air. It smelt of fresh equine sweat, canine saliva and poncey baldling aftershave. I was poised, the thoroughbred in the stall, the athlete in the blocks. I was the promise of unspent fury. As the first mutt broke into the clearing, his excitement erupted into howls of fearsome rage. I had time to see the baldlings that trailed behind Cerberus. They were a disappointing hunt, their once bright, red jackets were faded and moth eaten, the huntsman's horn was pitted and dull. These plastic aristocrats drunkenly bayed and laughed sounding no more cultured than the beagles that were pouring into the clearing. The huntsman blew his horn, I was off.

I streaked away from them, a debonair flash of orange and brown. Almost instantly the sounds of the hunt grew fainter. I was by far the better sprinter. My fresh, untired legs barely touched the ground as I ripped through the ferns and bracken. I easily dodged around trees, ran over hidden rocks and sprang off half-buried roots.

These were my woods and I knew every lump and bump. Even still, after just a few hundred yards that initial rush of adrenaline abated. My breath became heavy, weighing me down as it tore through my lungs. The hysterical barking of the dogs grew louder again. I dug in, keeping up the impossible pace that I had set for myself, but the dogs grew louder and louder. Every gasp of breath that wheezed through my chest tasted of canine rage. I saw what I was looking for, an over-grown monkey puzzle tree, choked with ivy, that had no natural place in an English woodland. I headed that way, turning at an angle that closed the distance between the hunt and I. The horses were among the hounds now and they galloped forward, vying for space. The baldlings that whipped them on cackled their delight and roared at one another. I could feel the hellhounds' breath on my back, feel their slobber drip on me. We burst out of the undergrowth, into another clearing. I eyed the terrain, finding the path Tweak and I had carefully marked out. I found one last reserve of energy. I shot forward and with a skip and a hop, jumping onto a semi-submerged tree trunk, then onto the ruined fountain that sat in the centre of what had once been a pond.

Do you remember how I told you about the Earl of Gumpton's ornamental gardens? This had once been a pond and at some point some infinitely wise fool had half-drained it and capped it off with wooden boards. Over time the boards had been covered with autumn after autumn's fall of dead leaves and they had rotted along with everything else leaving the most exquisite of traps. The hunt rushed forward, with their quarry now in sight and in the open they could taste blood. I stopped on the far side of the pond, pushing up a furrow of dirt. I turned to watch my master piece. The ground gave way with a satisfying crack under the combined weight throwing every dog, horse and baldling into the foul, black sludge below. They struggled in the mire, trying to get out. I laughed like a loon, gasping for breath and delighted at my own cunning. I put my claws in my mouth and whistled loudly. Bronson and Samson appeared, armed with the sharpened machetes I had procured. 'Fill your boots boys.' I chuckled as the pair of bodybuilders advanced, foaming at the mouth from the crystal meth I had also procured. 'The one who brings me the most scalps gets a bonus.'

*

While this these victorious events were taking place, Tweak and Mrs Frankie were in position. We knew that Mikhail wouldn't be watching my supposed downfall; he was blind. So where would the mole be waiting for news? He would be indulging himself in his favourite activity, having twisted, fetish sex with Saucy Sally. Tweak threw a nasty rodent bomb into one of Mikhail's tunnels, near to his lair. For those children of you who aren't evil, vicious bastards to small creatures, rodent bombs are the kind of chemical warfare agent that the world's governments have deemed too inhumane to use, unless it's against defenceless animals; or anyone who doesn't agree with neoliberal ideology. Within a minute of Tweak's deployment of the WMD, a strange, greenish smoke rose from the mole hill he had scraped away. A few seconds later Saucy Sally burst out into the daylight, her eyes were streaming and her paws were stretched out in front of her like she was a small, furry zombie. Just behind her was Mikhail, his pink fleshy nose was twitching like crazy and there was an old used condom tied around his throat. Tweak grabbed the end of the johnny and pulled him out into the open. Mikhail stumbled and fell to the ground with a small, pathetic cry. Tweak saw his opportunity and launched himself into the air, twisting and turning so that he landed flat on his back on top of the mole. A hundred thousand pins sunk themselves into Mikhail's soft flesh, piercing his unseeing eyes, shredding his sensitive nose and lacerating his body. Individually each wound was tiny, a miniscule scratch. Collectively they were agony. Mikhail screamed and thrashed around underneath Tweak. My hedgehog pal just laughed and wiggled himself around, driving each tiny skewer deeper and deeper.

Meanwhile, Mrs Frankie grabbed Saucy Sally around the throat, being careful to avoid her vicious claws and fangs, after all, she didn't want the AIDS. She cuffed the squirrel hard around the head, knocking her out, and then dragged her away from Mikhail's tortured screams, into the clearing in the middle of the woods. With a razor sharp claw Mrs Frankie scratched three huge gashes from the top of Sally's head and down her body. The squirrel awoke with a roar of pain but quick as a flash Mrs Frankie ripped and clawed and peeled Saucy Sally's skin off as if she were a twitching, bloody banana. She grabbed the squirrel by her skinless, purple tail and pushed it on to a sharp knot on the trunk of the old oak tree. Sally struggled and twitched and screamed and swore as she dangled upside down, very much alive. My Mrs Frankie was an expert eviscerateress, she had managed to avoid damaging any vital arteries or veins. The squirrel was a work of macabre art, worthy of that strange German, Dr Gunther, who gets a semi from playing with corpses.

After watching the boys working at the pond for a while I left them to finish off their job, I had one last detail to clean up. As part of their plans Clarence had unwittingly told Tweak just where he would be watching the day's events unfold, so I had arranged for Michael Mothins and his extended family to smear glue on every branch of the tree he had said he would use. I began to climb.

Clarence was just where I thought he would be. His feathers were ruffled from where he had tried to escape and one of his wings had become stuck to the branch as well as his feet. 'Easy now, Clarence. Sticking around for a bit?' I laughed at my own joke.

'Come on, Frankie. We could start again, we could be friends!' The crow squawked with desperation. 'I could help you out! I'm sure a clever fox like you could find a use for some eyes in the sky.'

I leant against the tree trunk for a moment, partly to regain my breath, partly for theatrical effect. Eventually I spoke. 'I think not, Clarence, my old mate.'

'Well then fuck you. What are you going to do? Bite my head off? Bring it on fox; I'm not scared of dying.' He cawed in a fit of rage. Flecks of crow spit flew from his beak and his dark eyes flashed with fury.

I shook my head and chuckled softly. 'Oh no my corvine chum.' My claws went to my red lippy which had popped out amidst all the excitement. I gave Little Frankie a few cursory tugs to get some blood flowing. 'You see, all this violence and terror does something to a fox, gets the pulse rate up. Did you know that us foxies have a penis structure called the bulbus glandis? It's basically a swollen knot that enlarges after penetration to ensure that foxy loving is not disturbed. It's also why vixens scream like they're being murdered.' I said conversationally. The look of horror in Clarence's eyes was worth the shame of fucking a crow.

*

Clarence's bloody, used corpse plummeted through the canopy of green leaves, splattering blood and fox spunk all around as it crashed into the dirt. I climbed down at a languid pace, stretching and enjoying my post-orgasmic victory glow. At the bottom of the old oak, Tweak was waiting with a joint for me. I took it from him and patted his back affectionately, getting mole-gore on my hand in the process. 'He's dead Frankie. I ground that little blind bastard right into the ground.' Tweak said.

I grinned and wiped my hand on my belly. 'Good work Tweak, thank you little buddy.'

Mrs Frankie approached me with a sultry smile and kissed me on the cheek. 'The squirrel's still alive, thankfully she's shut up now.' Mrs F gestured behind me and sure enough Saucy Sally was hanging from the tree trunk like a twitching Christmas tree decoration.

Just then Samson and Bronson appeared, covered in blood, mud and foul-smelling water. They still carried the machetes. This was the only possible wrinkle; these psychopaths had to be handled with tact and delicacy. 'Samson, old chap.' I said, calling him over. 'Did you know that your squirrel friend had a virulent case of the AIDS?'

The beavers face blanched and his eyes widened. His mouth fell open revealing his broken tooth. 'No…how do you…? Where ith that fucking thkank bag?' I could see the 'roid rage building in his face. Big veins stuck out in his wide neck and began to pulse and twitch.

'Don't you worry about it mate, we've taken care of her for you by way of thanks for your help.' I gestured flamboyantly at the tree and said a private little prayer.

Samson was silent for a moment. He watched what remained of his squirrel as it shuddered and trembled. He shrugged his shoulders. 'Cheerth for taking care of that Frankie.' He said before turning and walking away. Bronson nodded solemnly then followed his gym buddy. Meatheads.

By now, more of the residents of Gumpton Woods had gathered. They all watched from a respectful distance, finally regarding me with the awe and fear that I deserved. I stood up tall and puffed out my chest. 'Now here this.' I bellowed like the prince I was. 'Let it be known that those fucks who would fuck with me will have their shit shit all over. And anyone who puts that treacherous squirrel out of her misery will answer to me.'

Gerry the Catholic Caterpillar

Now, children, after all the excitement of the last story it is time for something peaceful to send you on your merry way. The hour grows long, as does old Frankie, so let's get this over with.

One cold morning in December, long after the dust had settled from the attempted coup, the animals of Gumpton Woods awoke with delight as they found that old Jack Frost had visited in the night and sprayed everything white with his magical stick. The pine trees were encased in a fragile crystal coat, autumn's fallen leaves had frozen to a brown mass that was not unlike a heroin ice lolly and in the pond Skibadee and Touché had to head-butt the icy surface just to get some air. However, even they didn't care when they saw how pretty and Christmassy the woods looked. 'Oh my,' said Skibadee, 'the trees are like silver statues.' Touché, as ever, said 'Meh'.

There was just one poor creature who didn't gaze with wonder at this enchanting scene, can you guess who it is, children?

Well I read you the title before we started, so if you can't then you're maybe a little retarded. Little Gerry the Caterpillar dragged himself through the frozen undergrowth, slipping and sliding as he climbed through frozen white brambles and leaves that were like ice-rinks. As he did, he muttered and tutted at all the joy and sin he saw around him. Bronson was gluttonising himself on a family of frozen earth worms; Bianca Bunny, who now had to work twice as hard to keep her daddy, was fornicating with every rabbit who could drag his cold little balls from out of the warren and Tweak and yours truly were hiding behind a tree and getting higher than giraffe pussy. Not that you'll find many giraffes around here, children, but if you did you'd find their pussies to be very high indeed.

Gerry had an unshakeable conviction in the truth contained within the bible, an inflated sense of self-worth and a petty arrogance towards any who hadn't found their way to the same God as he had. Like most people really, including atheists; but at least the religious have better parties. Why is there a Catholic caterpillar crawling through the woods? I hear you ask. Well, the only explanation I can offer is that Catholics get in some funny places; like choir boys or the Hitler Youth. A more pertinent question would be how a caterpillar came to be converted to such a bizarre anachronism as modern Catholicism? To answer that question, children, we need to jump back to a few days before this tale begins.

A hungover rat by the name of Big Dave had found himself in the church of Our Lady Of The Cross in the village of Whoreallygivesafuck. While poking around in the vestry he found an old, dusty box and several bottles of red wine. He helped himself to a hair of the dog from the wine while he scratched his small ratty head over the lock on the box. Fortunately his fingers were as nimble as a cockerel's cock and he popped the lock. Inside he found some dusty wafers that didn't look very appetising at all. Now, Big Dave was somewhat partial to rancid grease and chicken's ovaries from behind the local butchers but we'll eat anything once we're pissed, right children? He stuffed his cheeks with the wafers until his tongue was drier than an Alcoholics Anonymous Christmas party, then he necked a load more wine until it all made a pink mushy paste that dribbled from his mouth and stuck in his whiskers. Just then someone came into the vestry. Big Dave darted under a chest of drawers in the nick of time, dragging the box of wafers with him. An old priest came in, heralded by a smell of choir boys' fear that was quite over-powering. The old nonce shuffled around muttering and making a terrible racket. 'Now, where the bloody hell did I put that box of communion wafers?' Big Dave heard him exclaim. 'I can't have lost the body of Christ!' The priest uttered a dry chuckle and shuffled out, doubtlessly to over-charge old ladies for a place in heaven.

'Fuck humans and their bloody sky fairies.' Big Dave mumbled aloud. Now, the thought of eating the human messiah, even symbolically, made him feel a little queasy and he promptly threw up on the remaining wafers before sheepishly closing the box and slipping away. The vomiting made Big Dave feel a bit better, as a good chunder often can when we've been on the sauce, he retired to our fair woods so that he could recover in peace and maybe find Bianca Bunny for a spot of cross-species pollination. While he strolled along our furry friend coughed some sicky phlegm into the bushes where it landed on baby Gerry who had just hatched. Big Dave looked down at the poor caterpillar whose little eyes peered sadly from beneath his slimy secretion. 'What did you do that for, sir?' Gerry asked in a tiny, scared voice.

Big Dave was suddenly hit with an uncharacteristic flush of guilt. Suddenly inspiration was upon him. 'Well, little caterpillar, you've just been christened. That was the body of Christ, you're now a Catholic.' With that Big Dave strolled away, and out of this story forever. And there we have it, children; what a fucking idiot. Although to be fair, that is one of the better reasons that I've heard for believing in the sky fairies.

As Gerry grew and grew he dragged his faith with him like the burden that it was. His hatred for all things non-Catholic grew in him like a malignant growth until the joy of God had soured his heart and made bitter his life. His family disowned him, the other animals laughed behind his back and his friends avoided him like the ten plagues of Egypt. I never really wanted to point out to our poor, disillusioned Gerry that whatever crawls on its belly is described by the bible as an abomination; therefore our Gerry was himself an abomination. If God had made all creatures and he created something only to damn it, then maybe the big guy himself has a fucking screw loose, right children?

Anyway… We're back to our snowy morning in Gumpton Woods. Gerry had dragged himself away from all the happy woodland animals who were committing horrible sins such as throwing snowballs and erecting false idols they called snowmen. Deeper and deeper into the woods he went, into the shadows where used condoms were snagged in the brambles and only the bravest smackheads dared to venture. Suddenly Gerry saw a flash of red between the trees and then another. Hoping for a rabble rousing, Jew-hating performance of The Passion he picked up his pace, which is no mean feat for a tiny caterpillar. As he got closer he could hear grunts and groans that sounded like old men having a pillow fight. He pushed himself carefully through some leaves and into a clearing. What do you think he saw, children? It was Santa Claus and Jesus, that crazy Christmas double act! But what were they doing? Jesus was bent over with an irritating, serene look on his face that made you want to punch him, and Santa was behind him with his stupid, red trousers gathered around his ankles. Santa's face was screwed up and red, sweat rolled down cheeks and clouds of steam left his lips like he was a puffing steam engine as he groaned in a most un-festive fashion. His beard was stained nicotine brown and the noxious stench of stale brandy hung around him like a poisonous cloud.

Gerry cleared his throat, feeling a little uncomfortable. Jesus looked up in surprise and smiled benevolently. 'Hello Gerry. What brings you to these parts of the woods?'

Gerry was quite taken aback. 'How do you know my name?' He asked.

'I'm Jesus, God's my dad; I know everything there is to know. Now I hate to be rude, my small, many legged friend, but I'm kind of busy. Did you want something?'

'Um…I just want to know why you're letting Santa Claus bum you.' Gerry said. 'The bible teaches us that homosexuality is an abomination. Just like shrimp, pigs, tattoos, menstruating women and not wearing hats.'

'Ah, Moses certainly was in a pissy mood when he wrote Genesis. I always told Dad he was a little too militant.' Jesus replied wistfully. 'You are entirely right Gerry, gays are evil and must be burnt in the fiery pit. However, Dad struck a deal with Santa and now if he doesn't get to bum shag me once a year at Christmas time he won't bring people plastic reindeer that shit jelly beans or solar powered dancing flowers or electronic fish that sing "Don't Worry Be Happy by Bobby McFerran.'

'Ah, I always liked that tune.' Gerry replied, tapping all of his feet.

'Focus Gerry. Don't be a cunt.'

'Sorry Jesus.'

'If people don't get their fix of plastic crap once a year then they'd have no reason to believe in God at all, then the collection plates stay empty and the Vatican has no money to refuse to give to the poor. Mother Nature has to take one too, but she doesn't get anything out of it at all so I guess I'm lucky.' He didn't look very lucky to Gerry.

Just then Santa gave a particularly vicious thrust and his belly wobbled like a bowl of jelly. He pulled out of Jesus with a wet squelch and muttered as he pulled up his stupid red trousers. He let out an almighty belch that smelt of rotten fish guts. 'Ho, ho, ho, you fucking prick.' he bellowed as he leant against a tree to steady himself. 'See you again next year.' With that he staggered away through the woods. Remember children, if you're too well behaved that stinking old paedophile might come and visit you, so be sure to act up and be a bastard.

Poor Gerry was more confused than ever. 'But Jesus, if what you said is true then God has sold you out to make money from your birthday. How could anyone do such a thing? Surely our salvation is more important than crapping reindeer? Is God a hypocrite?'

The smug messiah smiled smugly. 'Strictly speaking, Gerry, you don't get salvation. Of all the creeping and crawling creatures on the face of the planet, God only applies to humans. It's in the small print. I'm guessing you're like most religious people and haven't actually read the good book? Just remember, Gerry, God moves in mysterious ways. We must not question him or the Christmas business model. Otherwise you're a heretic and could well be burnt at the stake by gibbering men wearing cassocks and speaking in tongues. The Christmas business model means that the heathen people in China can be fed a bowl of rice once a month while they provide good western folk with Ipods, Playstations and vomiting dollies; that people in Africa can be given jobs stripping their land of precious metals while smiling men with guns rape their daughters; and it means that fat western executives can grow fatter and fatter until they too are as obese and predatory as Old Saint Nick himself!' As he spoke, Jesus wiped his arse on a dock leaf and straightened his robes. 'Does that clear things up for you, Gerry?'

'Not really.' Gerry replied.

'Tough shit. Maybe you will understand when you are a wise, old butterfly. Or, if you're really lucky, you'll be reincarnated as a human one day. Don't tell dad I said that though, he hates Buddha.' Jesus said.

Just then a huge shaft of light tore through the bare branches high above, splintering into a billion shards and showering the woods with celestial silver. Jesus began rising, giving Gerry a most unholy eyeful of what was up his robe. He pointed at him and spoke in a voice that was suddenly very deep and Old Testament. 'Remember, Gerry, the Christmas business model must succeed at all costs. Especially if that cost is the health and happiness of non-Christians.' And so the son of the Lord ascended to heaven, one can only assume to sit in a darkened room and hug his legs while muttering about "feeling dirty".

Suddenly the woods were still and empty. Gerry was all alone with the snow and his thoughts. He felt enlightened, ready to face the world with renewed vigour and faith. He climbed up high on a bush so that he could see creation laid out before him. 'I wonder,' he said aloud to the silent woods, 'where can I find Tom Cruise's phone number? I want to be a scientologist.'

That's our Gerry children, he may be a cunt but we love him anyway, just as I love each and every one of you, even though you too are cunts. I do hope you enjoyed my tales, children. I'm afraid that now it is time for old Frankie to be off so I must bid you farewell. All that remains is for me to dispose of my pet writer, he has behaved so maybe it won't be too horrific an ending…

Remember children, stay out of the fucking woods.

The End

Printed in Great Britain
by Amazon